AF367330

# Toasted Orange Embers

Ketaki Mazumdar

BookLeaf Publishing

India | USA | UK

Toasted Orange Embers © 2024 Ketaki
Mazumdar

All rights reserved.

No part of this publication may be
reproduced, stored in a retrieval system, or
transmitted, in any form or by any means,
electronic, mechanical, photocopying,
recording or otherwise, without the prior
written permission of the presenters.

Ketaki Mazumdar asserts the moral right to
be identified as author of this work.

Presentation by *BookLeaf Publishing*

Web: www.bookleafpub.com

E-mail: info@bookleafpub.com

ISBN: 9789363310377

First edition 2024

*To all the amazing, talented, beautiful people who will find themselves in this book, for they too have given me comfort and courage.*

# ACKNOWLEDGEMENT

Gratitude is a powerful emotion. I warmly thank and celebrate my family, friends, colleagues, readers, and well-wishers who have helped me on this journey as a published author and poet.

I am indeed deeply blessed to have encountered so many. You are all a part of this book and my life.

Thank you, BookLeaf Publishing, for your writing challenge. This motivated me to write this book with excitement and joy.

# PREFACE

"Poetry is the spontaneous overflow of powerful feelings," said William Wordsworth.

Words fascinate me. I write poetry every day. The breeze, the sea, the greenery, the moon, and the stars are my muse. The elements and mood help me and vouch for the authenticity of these poems. They are all real.

Poetry for me is a celebration of emotions; it is wild, unpredictable, exulting, and fascinates me.

I write poems in free verse whenever the urge visits me…

I encourage readers to relax and read these poems, not in numerical order but by mood.

Open a page and let the poem empathise with you and excite you too.

I am there for you.

ketakimazumdar@gmail.com

# Table of Contents

# Quietness

unhurried
empty of time
or the agitations of youth…
…I just want to be…
look far into misty hills
watch the raindrops
on leaves

I have nothing more
to give you
nothing material or precious
except for the comfort of solace and peace…

I lay down the heaviness I carried
come to terms with sunsets
accept every change
enjoy the breeze on my face
let my inner wings lift…

be a part of
directionless
unhurriedness
between this now
and the ever after.

(c)ketaki mazumdar

# Bliss

You are the breath inside me...
the fragrance hidden, perhaps in the space...
between the conscious and the unconscious...
between the portals, I visit seeking...
the words of your eternal promises...
painted across the limitless sky.

In the mystical touches of the mortal and the
immortal...
between the mysteries of life after death...
and the deliverance of the soul...
as the body is left behind...
in a deep and final search...
for comfort...
for peace and infinite beauty...
I surrender the fountain of life...
fly to the bliss of death...
and the promised radiance.

(c)ketaki mazumdar

# Healing

Exquisite
the tenderness,
Your soft, whirling perceptions
that hold me gently...
like the breeze…

You flow through…
cupping the mogra flower...
holding safe all the petals...

You fill my fulfillment
with a sacredness… even as I dream...
I taste the nectar,
the rejuvenation…
the flowing spring of life.

I see again gardens of beauty
hear again the bird songs,

wonder at the stars and the new crescent moon's
timeless blessing...

In silken solitude
you unfold paths,
heal wounds with the balm of love…

When grey clouds gather,
when war strikes,
should I not dream of this healing…
gather petals of strength and hope,
find a realignment to life…
delve into a gratitude of quiet blessings…
as you lead me gently
to the beauty of the soul,
reveal subtly…
this conversation of healing.

(c)ketaki mazumdar

# Scents of Love

I smell their scents,
hear their soft, brushing melodies,
watch ethereal silver-grey streaked horizons
turn into magic shades...
haunting yet another monsoon,
on a canvas of seasonal triumphs…

the alluring fragrance
scents the familiar…
optimistic,
filled with promises,
emotions of softly unfolding love…
sparkled on raindrops...
on cusps of thoughts,
on luminous dreamscapes of my mind...
every cell tingled, draped
around the malhar music of nature's pleasures...
ghungroo beats fusion with
the flutter and excitement of sitar strings…

the shehnai's plaintive strains flow in the
whisper of a rain-soaked perfumed breeze...
the heart dances...
leaves fresh footprints of new memories...
discovers new creative journeys leading to
secret, deep discoveries...
tonight...
I feel uprooted,
sway like a night jasmine creeper drenched with
the magic of rain!

(c)ketaki mazumdar

# The Book

I could live forever
if you loved me
without the pain…
not in the pdf of a modern world
but in the actual...
printed and proclaimed…
The very form, size,
the texture of pages…
the blend of words by an alchemist,
the patterns
dearly thought out…
the hidden rhythms
the inner music,
the sacred threads in every page… dangerous
proclamations of mercurial truths…
said as is,
laid bare for the world to see…
penned with devotion…

ethereal voices that speak with softness or
strength…
nourishing... earth truths…
written with
deep roots
intimately weaving feelings...

love is dangerous
but oh so sacred
without artificial flavours…
sometimes written in solitude of longing but
belief of strength,
inherent energy,
primal, real, strong,
resonating with the age-old, the rustic, the earthy
and
the grounded… feelings I have and share with
you.

(c)ketaki mazumdar

# Thoughts

I curl up in the folds
of bleached, soft clouds…
will you tell me if I ask..
Why do I dig, so deep,
when beauty is on the surface...
to touch, to feel,
to see...

why do I watch a leaf
twirl and fall…
a flower drop,
a bird rise,
a mysterious butterfly flit and fly…
a woman suddenly shivers...

often, I slow down...
let colours of thought seep deep.
think of the breeze that shook the twig...
the fullness and heaviness,
the readiness of a flower to drop…

the final lift of bird wings,
the breath of a playful wind beneath the wings…
to make it rise in sweet victory…
I think and brood...
of a woman's shiver…
was it love
or because the fire is out...
sometimes I am like a raging, unsatisfied
forest fire…
trying to understand…
sometimes... just cold, cold ash of dying
embers...

(c)ketaki mazumdar

# Cornerstone

Sometimes a celestial
melody of sonorous chants
echoes within,
like the sound
of a prayer bowl…
a deep breath
of concentric rings…
submerging into
deep meditative realignments of realisations...
in a rediscovery of my ancient past life...
the touches my aura.

I revive in this secret cornerstone...
amidst the fragrance of pure incense,
the special aroma of oil in the diya...
the pink lotus clusters.

Every breath is fresh…

I breathe in the ages of omens and lessons,
wrapped
in a veil of eternity.

I thrive.
Balancing the clamouring world of today,
with the deep stillness within…
in serenity…
calmly
recharging cells,
that lifts me to the space of stars…
phosphorous glows… in an eternal galaxy...

Perpetual blooms of glowing mystery, spirit and
energy...
like enchanting bioluminescent forests, in
hidden earth corners and the aerial dome…
my cornerstone of radiance,
peace hues painted in my soul.

(c)ketaki mazumdar

# Textures of Love

In an infinite universe
we are the miracle…
I still believe in.

You are my spatial narration,
the metamorphosis of my internal secret dreams.

In this space of sky, sea, earth, air, ether...
wrapped in shawls of warmth,
I paint, pray and mould like a potter,
the texture of my life.
I'm rooted firmly, like a spreading banyan tree,
grounded… by love… the elements around
pulsing, nourishing, nurturing.

Here I breathe in life,
with faith,
in this precious space...
I reconfigure, interconnect, harmonise,
contemplate...

create the calm, the serene,
the sacred...
blend thoughts of
our hopes, our dreams…
weave our individual textures into a perfect
blend,
with soul togetherness, fragranced with peace.
We balance every churning whirlpool,
every shifting earthquake... with a resonance of
love and balance.
You and I keep the light safe… even though we
know,
love is vulnerable.
In this space, we are each other…
equal parts of a whole…
and here, together, we plant the seeds of love.
Here, we nurture the tunes of the unknown.

(c)ketaki mazumdar

# The Quest

I recycle pain
with sunshine and laughter…
somewhere like butterfly wings and dreams,
peeping from a pupa…

Joy does flutter through into sunshine glitter and
fragrances of colour burst,
full blooming Madhumalti creepers,
unborn rainbow colours inside approaching grey
clouds…
cotton trees bursting their pods…
as millions of cotton puffs
float with the breeze, as light as snow…
this parched summer.

Joy of the unexpected awes...
The Flame of the Forest, the Palash, the
Krishnachura...
the heavenly nectar,
interweave coolness in the parched...

there is a celebration... like the green mango
panna drink… minty, sweet and salty, quenching
our soul's dryness...

the birds sing…
I hang on to their music and secret code
language...
choreograph their words into the sacred dance.
I am unpredictable...
as I quest...
holding on to the sensual and the pain,
holding on to love, laughter, smiles,
the lost and the found feelings,
I breathe in myriad different ways...
smooth away the raw edges subtly...
I belong strongly,
part of a quest to
celebrate with intensity...

I'm part of each jigsaw piece,
a vagabond trying to make sense…
converting darkness into the source of light…
I belong with you to a human tradition,
a legacy...
of how to deal with life,
of how to deal with damage...

I will meet you here,
in the ordinary,

in trying to redeem wonder…
without apologising.
Stay with me if you want to…
depart if you have to.

c)ketaki mazumdar

# The Nomad

Every atom in me
came from the stars
blasted in a distant galaxy…
different parts of me, painted and filled with
sunshine, moon rays, asteroids, shooting stars
and glowing particles.
I glow differently at peak moments…
die blazingly into darkness…

sometimes wildflowers fill me,
promising blades of grass rise and sway…
I dance then
run, jump, whirl…
with music within me…

sometimes moon tides and currents push and
pull me…
I travel then…
to deep places, hidden caves, rolling deserts,
fluorescent ocean waves of emotions…

I create tsunamis of my own wildness...
birthing, dying,
curiously spinning and traversing…

my journey took untold generations...
now I am, where I am…
my limbs are wings,
my heart, a traveller,
my soul, a nomad…
I dance with you...
in a hundred different ways,
I walk your path…
on smooth sand, grit, pebbles,
river boulders, oceans and mountains...
I'm carried by the wind,
with embers burning…
fire, earth, air, water and ether…
You stir my soul to joyful searching...
with awe, wonder and magic,
searching,
believing.

(c)ketaki mazumdar

# With a Cup of Cinnamon Tea

Writings begin without warning,
amidst dust particles caught inside sunray
moments. Piled-up books totter uncertainly,
a spider in a sunshiny cobweb meditates.

All can wait as my pen scribbles with ideas that
can't wait...
racing with a butterfly on a garden windowsill...
parrots protesting,
sparrows twittering,
sunbirds diving with equal energy...

I breathe in the cinnamon tea...
write the last line of a poem from where you
covertly peep...
a few unfinished ones crawl, creep, slide in,
remind me to avoid too many metaphysical
revelations... while hummed mantras roll along

somewhere inside...
reflect colours from a cut glass bowl,
hidden deep within.

(c)ketaki mazumdar

# Today

Today I loved again...
when your footsteps made prints on the sand...
when the ocean swirled in,
when the frothy foam brought in magic
pearly shells and
left them behind on your footsteps...

From somewhere deep,
the ocean hummed...
the white seagulls stopped their swirling flight,
descended majestically,
tripped along your footsteps curiously,
joined your journey...

The last blush of the sun...
crept into the deep hollows of your footprints.
The reflections of stars soon parked in the
hollows, there...
amidst the Milky Way, foamy path and the
pearly shells,

I sat and watched…
as the sky dripped its seal of red...
the blue hour draped my shoulders, wrapped me
in feelings…
Today, I loved again.

(c)ketaki mazumdar

# Gypsy

She hides behind the mirror,
her light, a circle dome,
moon infused…
draped to the world with a message…
a message of personal non-existence.

The pseudonyms of her voice
are like swirls of smoke...
ascending their predictions from mysterious
woodsmoke...
she hides the true sound of her voice.

Broken and chipped the bells on her feet,
the beads of her necklace,
the swing of silver earrings, the crystal stone
rings…
feet cracked with travelling,
through high grass and jungles of dreams,

mists of desires,
dances of her life and soul, the inner cravings…
she is the beauty of this world,
the expanse of skies,
the ever-flowing bubbles in streams,
the woodfire smoke with hidden messages,
the wise old trees whose roots dig deep…
her abode.

The canvas of her life has myriad lonely
seasons...
solitary journeys with rain and storms...
she is hidden behind the mirrors of stars,
her soul filled with love...
her spirit feeling deeply...
she loves… fiercely and
her deep, dark eyes see what others don't...
her veiled words and face,
strike deep in others' souls...
words of music veils
her own inner self, she never reveals her Gypsy
origins.

(c)ketaki mazumdar

# Aligned Harmony

When distant drum beats throb in my heart,
when a reed flute sweetens my soul,
I crave extreme simplicity...
leave behind city bustle and a cluttered mindset.
escape to serenity. Paint a life of whites and
creams,
in shades of subdued minimalistic palettes... of
inward peace.

I paint my life in the ideologies of Kanso and
bathe in words of primal truths,
of neutral lights...
like the purity of a sun and silver moon,
the dawn light and dusk tones of a quiet life.
I paint the real spaces–a horizonless expanse...
of oceans, rivers and a forever sky... reflecting
life.

I cup pure raindrops and dew…

gather light that glimmers through... and pours
out between shivering leaves.
In a meditative stillness, hear the koels sing from
hidden depths.
I watch mesmerised a crane balance,
in peaceful stillness.

In the wall murals of my heart...
are reflections, the shadows of moods,
highlights of a pure energy that sustains,
complies with truth.
I balance in this tranquility,
aligned in nature's harmony of a space...
primal, inevitable, the truth of an inner peace
an attainable… Kanso beauty...
slow, serene, natural,
pure
aligned harmony.

(c)ketaki mazumdar

# A Search

I think today I surge like a wave,
from deep within,
billowing, gathering speed, cresting...
searching for the shore.

The sacred feminine is all around me…
an energy, an explosion
I explore,
searching for kindred spirits...
even as dappled sunshine strays in and touches
me…
perhaps blessing my search…

I link hands with the feminine…
unritualistic, undogmatic women who rise…
without conch shells blowing or beating drums...
whose souls rise free,

even as chained to mundane jobs and
responsibilities,
they quietly continue their mystic journey.
Living, loving, searching, meditating,
chanting,
journeying the essence of life...
unhermitlike...
they face the onslaught of time bravely.
They search, as do I...
we are conjoined feminine energy.

My unknown world is flavoured with women…
brave, multi-faceted,
understanding, empathetic and kind...
we share a deep journey beyond the surface.
Spirituality and holiness are as simple as a lotus
with a million petals...

(c)ketaki mazumdar

# Dark Phases of Sunshine

...and highlights of critical zones!
All I crave is in peaceful coexistence here,
of complex human nature.
Chance relationships
curated,
in peach colours of strong bonds of
Spring and Summer.

I drowse in the dark corner shadows,
sit on park benches…
and all I want to listen to,
are the voices of happy children and their
laughter.

I watch from here, the world changes colours
and
grow old with a calmness...
not begrudging love.

The race is on... in slow motion,

with abundant scars healing... but skin darkened
and wrinkled,
eyes that have seen too much,
half shut,
a heart slowly pulsing... that has felt and loved…
and lost.

I still wonder.
Imagine stars that journey around the world,
the ever-changing galaxy,
the uncertainty of a mystery called death.

In critical zones of existence…
I dream of world peace
seeped in beauty...
knock on my own personal world...
the meandering, flowing Ganga river,
snow-capped Kanchanjunga,
Nilgiri coffee plantations, unending stretches of
aquamarine oceans, magnificent foggy hills of
flowers, freshness and peace...
...the still unexplored tourist brochures, bursting
with wonders unseen.
On unspoiled golden dusky evenings of
ordinariness...
I think of quiet love, crinkled eyes,
secret smiles. Comfort, awe, acceptance of
fragrant jasmine blooms...
and gentleness.

Sometimes I wake up to nuances of letters,
words, verses,
lyrics of songs,
music and accompanying perfume...
remembering,
with quiet longing... then
sadly setting them free, releasing,
emptying oneself…
yet perhaps still waiting,
for love to find us...
again and again.

(c)ketaki mazumdar

# The Time is Right

My desert soul erupts…
the cascade of temple bells is a sudden surprise,
a reverberation of a symphony that
tingles,
vibrates and nourishes the soul,
wiping out hopeless, negative reasoning.

I stumble on divinity steps...
on tiptoe moments of discovery, while a
whimsical sun
removes darkness…
casts the black shadows
of abstract shapes,
on the dusty, crumbling walls of my soul.

The garden paths
lead to a myriad shades of green...
and freshness…

the vision of life seems to be washed clean.
Today I breathe hope.
I clutch on to all the musical notes... vibrations
of miracles! Now I know they
dwell in the dry desert of my soul too... unveiled
in bursts of glimmers, brightening dark paths of
despair with sacred
fragrances and music of morning prayers...
wafted in by the wind,
swirling, life around in buds of sprouting hope
and belief.
The time is right…
I merge today with that light…
with a brilliant butterfly in my soul...

(c)ketaki mazumdar

# Golden Days

Let's gather the dew from lillies...
It's that time of the year,
for freshness and imagination.

Let's wash away the smears of doubt and
darkness…
walk firmly on the bridge of a welcoming
tomorrow.
Let's release all regrets… collect instead the
light of strength in
the energy of golden sunflowers.
Let the red hibiscus
shake negativity and fear,
nurture the new Spring of hopes.
We can dwell now in a lavender consciousness
of purity...
cleansed by dew drops,
in a
rearranged world...

The sweet and sour berries and plums… of the
season, turn on the world...
Wake up...
to the morning sun's rays,
the singing wind uplifting the gorgeous,
vibrant kites…
dancing, diving, pirouetting in the blue skies.
Let's gorge on healthy sesame seeds bound with
the season's first molasses…
as the Sun transits... into Capricorn... the longer
golden days of
prosperity
denoting fullsome harvests.

(c)ketaki mazumdar

# Ochre Afternoons

Somewhere a crow
caws desultorily.
In the lost codes of a burning Indian noon,
there is a cavernous pause...
the stillness of a spreading heat decides to give
up and just nap.

The solitude of fevered ennui,
makes flowers and leaves droop listlessly...
the hot ochre sands stop blowing in unruly puffs
and
curl up beside a green sea,
the beach grass is hypnotised to an unwavering
stillness.

A hungry seagull circles slowly,
in apathy, in a
desolation of heat...

awaiting the breaking of the noon fever...
for an evening breeze to cool and refresh...
awaiting the heaty day to crumble deliciously
into a butterscotch,
orange and strawberry syrupy sauce...
with some dollops of white ice cream clouds
on a dark, rich brownie,
flambéed dusk sky.

(c)ketaki mazumdar

# Textured Tapestry

There is a texture to memories...
Patterns of beauty...
A longing to be felt...
and to be understood.

Truths are embroidered here, without
pseudonyms and masquerades...

Strange how this sliver of a new moon looked at
me...
reminded me of the half-moons on your
fingernails,
of how the slightly nippy November breeze
ruffled your hair...
framing your face...
momentarily...
how the romance of dragonflies mysteriously
fluttered by...
warning me, perhaps of rain.
How the iridescent blue stars paused…

matching our silence.

Unheard dialogues and
nuances crossed borders with us...
but only I returned… to keep promises.

You were the visual narrative
that became a texture,
in a tapestry of memory… in a sky of
disappointed sapphire...
and the reality of a stunted moon...
no matter how beautiful.

You were the texture I touched…
a dewdrop on rose petals…
carrying rainbows of love
on pages of a love poem…
just a weave...
on a memory.

(c)ketaki mazumdar

# In Gratitude

You will find me curled under trees,
sunlight gold filtering gently,
listening to life's melody.

I maximise my soul in this surrounding beauty,
drenched in the true natural colours of earth…
unpretentious, honest
and holy...
in palettes of browns, tans, blues and a million
shades of cool greenery.

My soul seeks the minimalist… and I learn to
hold life softly...
and let go gently...
I learn from nature's rules,
try to be like the breeze… just passing through.

This life, I know, is a borrowed garden…

bounteous and magnificent…
here we take turns to become dust…
I accept and let the spirit of gratitude touch my
soul...
for this entire magnificent galaxy is woven
beautifully in time...
we are a blessed part of this heritage,
in a deep connection to precious
space.


(c)ketaki mazumdar

# Dreams Sold

She is Art and she is Life…
For me, the glorious native flowers and
the dark, rich clay…
remind me of fragrances and colours of tribal
womanhood and innocent life.
The resounding sounds of drums and energy!

Adivasi women of our country, draped in natural
colours of brightness,
nose rings gay,
oiled, dark hair decorated with flowers that
match their mood...
Beauty surrendered to grace…
in the curves of their taut, healthy bodies.
Bangles jingling,
ears studded with jewels of nature.
Shells, seeds, flowers and feathers round their
necks.
Anklets of beaten silver… on dark velvet skin.

Beautiful dark eyes of excitement that call out to
life...
flashing white teeth and smiles.

Under orange and red Mahua flowers of a heavy,
springy summer...
a flaming flower tucked in her coiled hair…
She represents the wild beauty of freedom and
nature.
Dancing and singing in unison…
uninhibited!
Like Palash and Simul blossoms...
too often abducted and crushed by careless,
greedy hands and feet.
In innocent vulnerability... who will protect them
in their time of need?

(c)ketaki mazumdar

# Shadow Zones

Sometimes, with the permission of the twilight
hour...
intense on its own perfection journey,
in seamless rhythms...
the vibrant carpet of nature is rolled in...

The birds fly home,
the touch-me-not leaves curl inward,
the lotus stands silent... petals tightening…
I look inwards with a strong bonding,
with the twilight sky...
secret edges smudging to shadow zones...
descending, drowning darkness
gold flicked,
locked in feelings and visitations…
and the protection of guardian angels...

Multiple expressions surround us,

as the lamps are lit...
glowing aura moments flood the flesh and the
spirit...
Indecipherable depths on faces,
the poignant smoke of incense gently touching
closed eyelids,
in gratitude and praise.
Cascades of overlapping lapidary waves,
intrinsic beauty engraved
in nature's magic hour, an hour of inner
illumination.

(c)ketaki mazumdar

# Tears on Chinar Leaves

Lovers' sighs escape in sorrow.
Heartaches are silenced under the shade of
Chinars.
Each morning, a familiar silhouette hovers in my
mirror for we are
connected, you and I with dew drops on sunlight
and tears on moon rays…
and the kangri vessel that embers our warmth.

We are a part of a self-destructive temporal
dance,
in metaphors of hope...
tinged with frost,
despite the march of guns,
chattering, defying death.
We are connected... with music and weaves of
lotus stems and delicate blooms...
shikaras ferrying Spring... almond blossoms,
summer fruits and bright, autumn chinar
leaves...

I reflect on sharing with you... desires in a safe
space,
in a morning light that however aches...
in this dew-dripping autumn... our words are
hidden, not spoken or exchanged...
we talk instead of birds and flowers, sow seeds
lovingly for gardens of beauty...
but never reach each other's soul hidden deep for
fear of separating.
Our fingers never touch or feel our warmth... or
decipher feelings always hidden in laughter and
tears.
Loss is too fierce, as is pain…
reality is too large and time
too dear, too precious.

In a shikara covered with lotus blooms, we are
nestled but doomed…
eyes open to a world of distrust.
We are awake till acceptance makes us sleep,
and the beauty of snowflakes covers the lake in
an unreal, pristine white.

A war rages for possession of silhouettes of
deodar trees, heavenly flowers, walnuts,
almonds, apples and saffron…
Helpless lovers and families migrate,
dwindling...

disappearing...
as yet… something in me still wants to live,
to twine fingers and caress rosy cheeks, sing of
love ghazals and togetherness...
tenderly...
wipe the tears from Chinar leaves.

(c)ketaki mazumdar

# To Just Be

Often at dawn,
a yearning creeps over me like a silent, soft
drape...
to create,
to touch beauty,
in a moment of silence and intimacy.

My poems are all feelings,
sensitive, tentative…
moss-grown truths,
deep, living emerald.
My poems are birds in flight against the dawn of
lavender and pink sunrise...
in amazing celestial flights...

Motionless is my heart, as the moon climbs and
takes her place,
invisible behind a cloud screen...

beauty hidden behind leaves and twigs of a
statuesque tree draped in memories…
motionless and watching.

Thoughts of aching beauty of different colours
gather...
words behind empty doorways greying with tints
of autumn brilliance…
dry red leaf splashes meaning, and dew drops
glisten on grass.

I watch, mute, still,
gathering palpable words in time frames…
I hold, see, touch, just be...
gazing with pure eyes that pause upon unknown
worlds.
The wind shapes fascinate…
the stars dissolving, silences the aura of
gathering darkness in corners…
where silent lands are hidden in purple shades.
I quest there...
...to just be.

(c)ketaki mazumdar

# Intimacy

the smell of wet earth and mogras in a bowl...
the heady fragrance of rose attar and sandalwood
smoke, incense, marigolds and lilies...
smouldering eyes and mysteries...

the hair entwined with jasmine garlands...
lotus-shaped eyes,
the freshness… of flower petals and tumbling
hairpins,
dew drops of sweat... on warm skin
gleam...
in the lamp light beam,
as pupils dilate and widening eyes meet...
fingers interlock,
a tiny touch in a sudden explosion of feelings...
moments pulse with unknown surprises.

(c)ketaki mazumdar

# Healing Colours

desert dunes gently undulating
painting toasted orange the sand and the sky…
here an amazement of reflected embers glitter
like gems in the sand...
a mirage
dazzling…
a golden glory of hiddenness
reaching the empty horizon...
it's here where the wind blows hot and cold...

I follow the unlaid trail,
searching and
asking the self
for answers...
wondering at this mystery,
this ceremony of nature…
this toasted orange carpet glowing,
this caravan of camels

holding high their heads...
as if they knew it all…
silhouetted regally against an orange haze of a
mysterious sky...

I hear the tinkling bells… like ribbons of music
that I follow,
coloured threads floating like spirits,
woven rugs glowing warmth on their regally
humped backs...
unerringly walking to their destination of
answers... the life-giving green and blue oasis,
a place for rest, retreat, recuperation and
revelations.

I carry a sacred burning in me...
a hope for answers to this existence...
in the stillness of inner silence...
in this spiritual world of prayers...
I wait for your answers here…
here, where even water is hidden...
but here, the soul is unpolluted, living,
waiting with the answers...
amongst these toasted orange embers...
to rejuvenate and quench my thirst.

(c)ketaki mazumdar

# The Crimson Ode

captivating yet eluding captivity...
beauty that glows in each beholders gaze,
change…
times eternal state and heady sweet fragrance…
the crimson blooms are a part of a game,
challenging, captivating beauties,
finding their own life force...
did the Universe conspire to bring together this
beautiful energy… petalled flames that glowed a
hidden love story…
soul dancing in the breeze happily,
while drunk, bemused multicoloured gems of
butterflies kissed
their deep soul pulse.
The crimson petals bloomed in strength,
embraced their joy.

Love bloomed within the crimson…
the butterflies scattered their blessings…
spread them wide on sultry afternoons,

spread them on spring days and in the rains.
An abundance of beauty spreads into a maroon
carpet…
in a visual, soul symphony…
crimson blossoms of eternal love vibrancy.


(c)ketaki mazumdar

# Some Legends Still Breathe

Strong women who are gentle,
Fierce women who are compassionate,
Scarred women with beautiful thoughts.
Unschooled women whose knowledge is vast...
who are path-breakers and
downtrodden women with immense resilience.
Single women, so
successful and happy with life.
Unloved women with love in their souls.
Uncared for women who deeply care for the
downtrodden.
Abused women who are resilient...
Small-town women who rule the world with
global intelligence and the
determined women, who are now legends.

(c)ketaki mazumdar

# Opium Dreams

let spicy scents
delusive joys
opium dreams...
fill me today…

before life gets darker
hazy
hair sparse and white, cropped carelessly...
before staggering steps are unsteady,
the mind confused…
wavering
wandering
aimlessly

let me find today
a place of joy...
let me give birth to some poetry
to be read and remembered
loved
before I am forgotten...

let me write about happiness... starshine and a
luminous space called Heaven...
get lost there today
before fatigue overtakes destiny.

(c)ketaki mazumdar

# Indian Summer Noon

The crumbling red
heritage mansion sighs,
the old green-painted shutters
let's in slats of dusty light, heaty sun strips glint
on the mosaic floor...
on my red and white mulmul sari,
on a bowl of cut cucumber sprinkled with salt
and pepper, soaked in lime.
I sip from a cool, sweet coconut...
even as my body sweats... salt drips...
equations of emotions to an Indian Summer
noon heat...
I listen,
embraced by this noon stillness…
to the insistent cry of a koel,
as if there is no end to our untrodden dreams...
our souls weep...
eternity becomes an epitome this summer noon.

A breath of mogras soaking in a bowl…
embraces fragrances of languid half-awakening
and sleep.

The frozen marble statues stand in repose on
round tabletops,
the unlit red Belgian glass wicker lamp
stands witness to eras...
a Harmonium that once played Tagore melodies
has a dusty cover...
an empty porcelain vase misses the
Rajanigandha blooms,
Ghungroos are tumbled on red velvet…
piled up books are scattered,
a white conch shell of cool beauty is on a brass
plate...
Life flows here...
even in noon stupour...

(c)ketaki mazumdar

# Still…

my mind races
even though time stands still...
my thoughts are with you, still…
your eyes twinkle, like mischief dew,
still, we walk the beach together, fingers gently
touching…
still, our shoulders brush…
we are draped with moon ray magic.

Still…
we find sunlight neath dark clouds,
still... mix emotions, colours, feelings…
still tingle,
still dance,
still merge with sunsets, dawn, dusk...
autumn rain, spring and snow...
still blush,
still trust,
still whisper words of love,
still respond to each other's calls,
still... like the tide

our pull is strong...
and still...
...we believe in the strength of love.

(c)ketaki mazumdar

# Your Touch

On an apricot and peach-tinged day,
will you reassure me of my worth...?
Will you reassure me that my wings can catch
the sunlight's glow,
that I can soar and flow?
That you will always hold me safe?

I have been told,
that in me is the cure.
All things broken need my touch,
with the gentle art of Kintsugi
sealing flaws and cracks with molten
gold, healing.

Why then do I seek to lay on your chest,
find the healing in the nape of your neck...
find the resilience in your arms...
find the caring,

the melting point…
fulfilment is there.

Apricot and peach tones of soft, flushed warmth
are there.
I burrow there like a glowworm seeking a home.
I spill here
apricot and peach-blushed joy.

(c)ketaki mazumdar

# Primal Soul Dance

The internal music touches my soul.
I dance with joy, often alone.
I watch the spring bloom,
apricots and cherry blossoms,
Revel in their soft, pure beauty.

In the passion of falling rain,
pure and fragrant jasmine blooms,
I dance with you,
in an onset of romance and love rhythms.
Under the flowering Kadamba tree,
I'm showered by fragrant petals,
while the heavy full moon smiles.
I hear the sound of the sweet flute…
I soul dance with you.

Like wildflowers, my soul dances with abandon,
Rippling in the balmy breeze,
I am like a happy, tiny sunbird,
Diving, pirouetting, gliding

Enthralled with this world,
Created by you.
In the ecstasy of dawn, dusk and hope,
In a trance…
I spiral dance…

To rhythms divine, heard only by me.

Like the undulating ocean waves
speckled with glittering sundrops,
My soul dances with joy.
I sway and whirl to a beat as old as time,
As simple as the bells of a windchime,
My soul dances,
to the wonder of a moving galaxy.
In an ecstasy of love, hope and eternity,
Like a tiny, happy humming bee…
Chasing the honey of divinity…
I transcend my soul,
in a primal dance of ecstasy.

© ketaki mazumdar

# The Waterfall

She is a credence in poetical assonance…
in communion with my soul.
Each drop of silver sings in unison…
a choir of sweet power.
I listen, entranced, to the birds and the luscious
ferns,
The wet rocks, the pebbles tinkling, the
drumming,
my wet hair and the wind's wet, swishing songs,
play their symphony, vibrating every cell.
Ragas and crescendos, like waves of musical
innuendoes…
splash joyfully on me.
I listen to the musical pace, their innuendoes, the
overtones of nature…
in soft beats,
they blend into my heart…

the sound groups on leaves, twigs, branches and
flowers create earthly music.
A rushing current of musical notes and rhythms,
hangs on silver strings,
like a harp playing celestially to my very being.
My desert soul erupts
with this cascade of silver bells.
God-given music!
Splashes of joyful abandon transform
into a rainbow of awe.
The Jal Tarang plays magical notes of ascending
and descending sweetness in perfect
transformations.
Mist to spray to light sparks to magic…
mixing sounds naturally in a glorious free-fall of
cascading joy.
The waterfall tumbles,
shooting sprays like strings of the sitar…
playing their lightning magic.
My feet dance lightly on rippling waves of
sounds.
The sighing in pine trees, the tinkling, the
whistling, the bubbling,
all the voices of nature pour their feelings into
my heart.
Here, I stumble on divinity!
The awe, the wonder, the outpouring music of
purity.

There is peace in this symphonic, rapturous overture
of inherent, unorchestrated, freedom,
of soul-stirring musical sounds…
A waterfall's ecstatic symphony.

(c)ketaki mazumdar

# The Boatman

Lonely wafts the boatman's song on the Ganga
River.
I hear, in the silence of the night,
the reflected musical moonlight,
the rhythmic splash of the oars,
the yearning mystic voice,
the sweet melody.
The white Kaash flowers swish and sway,
the moonlight ripples and dances…
to subtle, unknown musical rhythms.
Somewhere in this open vista
I connect with stars, galaxies and planets, spread
in wondrous trails.
I connect with celestial manifestations,
the subtle music of immensity!
Eternity of musical notes that touch the
'forever'.
The secret sounds of the Universe open its doors
and windows…
calls to you and me.
Touches our spiritual journey.
I hum its praise in meditation… in a song of
reverence…

from the core of my soul.
Such a power of mystery, resonance and rhythm,
in the dimension of an aura… I merge in Meraki,
drown in the slow rhythm of planets…
Like the tuning fork of spirituality, I touch the
high and low notes…
of an inherent nostalgia.
I float on gentle waves and ripples of spatial
music,
tune into that sensitivity… in deep reverence.
I feel the musical surge of purity in my
accepting heart,
open the windows of my soul,
indulge my needs in fulfilling the desires of the
music,
like a gentle wafting of a chiffon veil.
I breathe and tingle in a floating harmony, and I
play your tune.
I vibrate to your unwritten, evolving music…
in a free rapture of Sur, I swing in rhythm.
My earthly soul heals wrapped in musical
notations
with the musical tones of celestial love.
Unheard, unchartered, I soak in the heavenly
clouds
of those lavender blues.

(c)ketaki mazumdar

# Palash Blooms

A playful gust blew in
The wind's breath rained on me a shower
Of scarlet Palash blooms.
I breathed in
Let the colours soak my soul,
My day transformed with joy
Was blessed
As down they drifted.
In my sudden laugh
Was a dare
In my soul
The red guided seal
Left it seems…
God's blessings.

(c)ketaki mazumdar

# I Respond

The world tried to weigh me down
With its one-way road
Its rules…
There is a restlessness in me
I do not
Want to follow a readymade handbook
This is my secret, authentic truth

There is such joy
To cross thresholds…
And float freely in this world

I walk and sing under stormy skies
Visiting rituals and beliefs
Yet follow the path of winds and clouds
The sun and moon's mystic journeys.
My soul dances, prays,
Heals with vitality
A positive force surges
Untrodden new vistas

Fresh paths open up for me.

I respond to every cell
That says… Live!
The river in me
Moves exultingly…
This I know, is your ordained truth
My response to my destiny.

(c)ketaki mazumdar

# Kolkata Depictions

While you stood in your white sari,
the red border, blazing…
with the red bindi and the
red sindoor, marking its trail...
wet, long hair open to the sun...
a niche beauty
just married...
made for love…
with the heavy touch of gold bangles, necklaces
and tinkling gold balas…

You smelt fresh and fragrant...
like the gold champa buds... linked with trust...
ready for a tryst in the paradise of newness...
as yet unconquered,
young nubile
spirit still confident,
flying high with the beauty of youth.
You dripped… cool water drops from your long,
black hair…

and a dampness spread alluringly at your slender
waist...
You shivered as the sun blazed away...
and the cold winter wind blew...
charcoal and woodfire cooking buckets blazed...
to fry the dinnertime finely slivered potatoes and
white luchis in pure ghee...

wicks tended,
hurricane kerosine lamps were lit... and there
was a golden glow.
In the puja room, the earthen lamps of purity
glowed...
You rang the tiny brass bell...
moving energy to ward off evil...
every dark corner spread the fragrant loban for
protection...
your kajal-lined eyes looked at the world with
innocence and a newborn purity...
and the beginning of maturity and responsibility.
Covering your head, you bowed to the deity and
prayed for your new family's blessings...
The white conch shell was blown thrice...
reverberating energy.
Gently, your soft, red alta feet walked on tiptoes,
danced... on air!

(c)ketaki mazumdar

# This Too Shall Pass

I am the transient dew drop.
The island, half submerged, floating in the sea.
The tree that blooms,
and then sheds its flowers and leaves.
I am that gushing stream, rushing.
Made with melting ice, fresh and pure, pristine,
then turning brown and muddy, silting and
stopping.
I am the Seasons, birthing and changing,
evaporating,
like a soul's journey...
Changing forms and draping bodies.
I am the ashes carried by the winds.
I am the ruins of a glorious might, of what was
and now is gone,
like the curtains raised,
but must fall.

I am the clenched fingers that must relax.
I am that Time...

must move on.
Impermanence paints magical illusions of
colourful dimensions.
The poet paints and strings words,
to reclaim the impermanence as much as
possible.
The unfinished voyages of the heart...
The saddest impermanence... Is love.
For it is decreed... this too shall pass,
        except when written by a poet, in words.


(c)ketaki mazumdar

# Fire and Ice

master narratives of the body,
sometimes like lily pads…
opening, uncurling, unfolding, in the moon and
shine,
like the sky reflecting in their soul...

like a woman in flames and ice,
knotted up in the reality of daily life...
graceful imitations of death drives in dark
tunnels...
searching for light...
the blue beyond unreachable...

yet reaching for the peach apricot... when love
was alight and softly warm
fingers intertwined in sweet ripeness...
a master narrative,

a body shaped, now in retreat... bitter bites into
low depths,
mystical rides of this world...

it's still a sunlit morning... a narrative in gold
and blue...
overflowing jasmine in bowls, in such fragrant
delicateness... yet...
yet just not the same…

stars shine at night,
leaves aflame in autumn...
a mirage that smokes, curls up on forest floors,
narratives reel of infinite age...
the fire and ice of a preordained symmetry of
life...
beautifully uncurling…
bonded with heat and cold.

(c)ketaki mazumdar

# Kolkata in My Blood

Sometimes I chase fireflies
stare into dark eyes, searching for truths
unfolding...

the fireflies are impatient...
like wildflowers, even as the sun sets
they yearn for another morn of joy…
tonight, distant rain perfumes, silence
settles…
there is an uncertainty and restlessness as dark
clouds gather and fragrant mogras brew a storm
in me...
music of the city soul lingers...

The city of joy sleeps restlessly
hiding her own stories…
the Goddess of the city watches…
the Ganga is lit with boats... flows its myriad
journeys...
human, spiritual, celestial...

drawn by rickshaws…
the pulse of this city throbs and lingers...
in its arts.

Reflected in my prayers are broken brick walls,
crevices of ages and marbles of mansions…
shooting stars insist on wishes.

The oil lamp in my soul glows,
I hear the flutter of the city in firefly wings…
a delicate interweaving of immense beauty...
and helpless veins of pain…
sometimes I chase fireflies,
overwhelmed by their beauty and mortality,
a passionate rapture and the law of life...
rapture and the inevitable.

(c)ketaki mazumdar

# Ageing

Rose-coloured filters age...
I search
for serene, calming retreats
of tranquility...
cool, calm
stillness... creepers that bloom,
spreading trees that shade... comfort.

Summer youth blinds.
I search
an ambience to calm my soul from the intense
and the passionate...

I search
in nature's timeless elegance,
an intimate setting,
a tranquil space of
understated aesthetic appeal...

custom sculpted with empathy
for you and me…
solace in the depth of wind-sculpted autumnal
years…
to unravel
our many decade's journey…
from secrets of summer strawberries, angel
kisses,
red cherries to winter crunchy apples...
mild days,
juxtaposing and harmonising our personal
mysteries...
demystifying spirituality,
revealing all to each other...
This new summer solstice...
we melt into each other in ageing
harmony.

(c)ketaki mazumdar

# Koelidi's Bakul Tree

The veil of a warm summer evening settles
slowly
and the echo of the Bakul tree sings
above the sound of a sonorous wind chime,
a miraculous celebration of nature conducts a
symphony…
an original musical masterpiece... permeates,
crosses walls, windows poignantly.

I introspect, woven in a shawl of bird songs,
designing dreams...
of their days of adventurous survival…
now they fly homeward and live as a democracy
of happiness…
In a rising crescendo of perspectives
they chatter and talk
create a weave in my mind,
a buzz of joy at nature's immensity and
subliminal mystery…

I delve deep inward into stillness…
the energy is in the aura of exchange all around
before night settles its illusory mantle…
do the avians discuss their memories of making
homes, joy and loss, life and death...
in murmurs of connectedness and silken
dreams...
or are they just human fragments lush with
imagination...
in the resonance of a Bakul tree over numerous
decades...
alive with sounds, twitters, togetherness,
the birds share a home here free of rent,
amongst leaves and fragrant flowers…
they communicate... respond to a universe of
consciousness.

I steal secluded moments of the aroma of a
deeply personal experience...
the warmth of hospitality... the romance of
compassion...
I sit in a pristine home of abundant history,
photographs,
tall porcelain vases, marble artifacts
and gentle caring...
I awaken gratefully to generosity…
given so spontaneously.

(c)ketaki mazumdar

# Song Waves

I'm often lost in songs.
Scattered in the wind
are notes attached to strings…
pulled by colours of feelings.

I'm part of a landscape
in a fistful of sky...
green rolling hills and sighing forests,
splashes of blue-green oceans merging with a
golden beach,
aromas of incense in temples...
rising crescendo and symphony.
Red tilak blessings, like soaring music, dancing
on my forehead.
Embedded notes
deeply entrenched in spirituality.

Song waves touch the sun's rays and moon
paths, reach the stars...
sometimes my songs reflect on tender, deep
gazes…
singing untold tales.
I write words and notes,
paint pictures with brush strokes that drip
music...
wondrous feelings merge, drift,
slow dance...
nuances, float in guilded pools of notes... silver
and gold...
dipped in maroons and blues…
and musical mood swings.

(c)ketaki mazumdar

# Cinnamon

The earth and sky are melted cinnamon blends
that delight me.
I watch with awe the unfolding cinnamon dust,
the scented bliss.
Myriad hues whispered in an oasis of cool
dusk…
Deep thoughts filtered,
meandered, levitated to the galaxies above,
into impetuous spaces of the mind,
whispering to the heartbeats,
in the language of the Universe.

Tranquility, pulsations of sweet truth,
stirring of cinnamon dust…
a landscape of hidden beauty...
that only a woman can see...

Hazed landscape of airy distances fading into
dew-washed residual pale blues and purples in a
reappearance of romance...

A quarter of heaven is an expression of love
where a silver moon rules…
My hair flutters,
tinted by the gleaming moon rays...
a tropical balmy breeze full of cinnamon dust,
collaborates with tender vulnerability in my
soul…
intensely... purely alone, alone, butter-soaked
and drunk
in the vanilla essenced cinnamon world of love.
Here I surrender… in this secret place.

(c)ketaki mazumdar

# Holding On, Letting Go

On this day that invites grief...
I weave together... change and silent fear,
Loss and hope,
vulnerability and self-discovery...

Mundane thoughts flow with the profound...
endless summers of flowers and hurricanes of
destinies.

I hold on to trees I see, without leaves,
all ablaze with vibrant floral glory…
I hold on to hope…
like a simple glowing earthen lamp I see,
spreading light...
even as the sky is covered with a duvet of grey
and black print…
I hold on to a fistful of river earth...
from here, I know a living plant will grow...

I hold on to the simple beauty of a bird song…
for that uplifts my soul...
I hold on to life lessons learnt from all my
teachers...
hold on to the balance of holding on and letting
go...!
I hold on to awe and wonder...
for from here I know…
miracles are born.

(c)ketaki mazumdar

# There is no Rush

I cling to earth's breast,
paint murals of her abundance...
feel her eternal comforts,
her ephemeral colours,
the warmth of her birth,
the delicate shades of green ferns,
the shivering green peacocks,
the tumultuous creepers
the dance of wildflowers...

I cross and recross boundaries,
collect sweet and sour berries,
pin flowers in my hair,
unabashedly,
whisper my pledge to be free...
live only in beauty,
drown delightedly in aromas searching their
source...
swim in pure crystal rivers...

chase dragonflies, be hypnotised by fireflies,
laugh at crossing boundaries,
sing legends and myths,
know they were of my human tribe...

as pen scratches paper,
night insect songs penetrate mists...
on rain-soaked nights,
the surround sound of life seems far away...
the elements are a witness to beauty...
here, outside the chatter,
but deep in her heartbeats,
I witness introspection,
inhale life and beyond,
touch stars,
know the Universe is mine...
like a shadow, I belong to you,
follow your footsteps...
even as fresh, wet earth and myrrh mingle in me.

(c)ketaki mazumdar

# Angels

Angels do not always
have wings...
or be there only
when we say our farewells…

Angels can be ordinary humans
not only luminous, except in their secret
kindness...

Tomorrow may start without you or me, when
vulnerable, bewildered and lost...
we all could encounter an angel… sitting on the
edge of a rock...
on dark nights or staring into a flickering
flame...
perhaps rocking at a party…
with a feeling of aloneness...

Angels surprise us… on hospital beds,
while burning with fever,
while walking lonely roads,
or huddled under torrential rain…
having no friends who cared enough…
to give shelter.

Time, I know, is finite,
despair, pain, joy, helplessness all
minuscule journeys in no man's land...
in that sudden lurch...
in my heart...
an angel may visit...
knocking silently on closed doors...
they are the turning points…
out of nowhere...

when touched by an angel
unknowingly,
touched by a peace,
amidst fury,
making special an ordinary story...
believe then in Angels…
they are there.

(c)ketaki mazumdar

# A Knock

Serendipitous yearning,
transcending space...
my knock is
subtle…
on God's hidden gate...
with fingers of some urgency…

…for strangely, whether in a coffee shop,
a temple of historical treat,
a dinner party…
or when old friends meet,
or on a garden bench
beneath trees...
facing rolling mountains,
calmed by a cool breeze...
I live a life of
disconnect
a mixture,
a confusion,
a jigsaw of paints...

the whole of me
I offer to God...
the sane,
the calm...

we all,
I know, search for that last home…
connect there deeply…
like roots clutching Mother Earth...
You reveal without a word
that I am your descendant,
we share a wall,
a membrane of life,
of inner and outer dialogue…
You nurtured my growth...
now I yearn to return home to your
immense eternal space,
your loving, caring grace.

 (c)ketaki mazumdar

# When Birds Fly Home

Echoing the changing leaves,
brushed so sensationally
from temptingly fresh
to burnished gold,
to lifeless…

a forever love
a cosmic symphony
an eternity...
while it lasted...

like the smeared residual
shimmer of peeled nostalgia in the crevices and
veins…

did we exchange souls and heartbeats... pulsing
from moment to moment?

In a spectrum of loss, I exhaled...
shed,
like the leaves,
the aromatic for the mundane... trying to survive
change...
while evening colours changed...
and the birds flew homeward.

(c)ketaki mazumdar

# The Healer

On days like this,
when nothing makes sense,
You lift me.

On these darkest of nights and days of turmoil,
rolling dark, speeding clouds and lightening,
You never let go of my fingers…
calm every fear of drowning… of being lost
under
turbulent waves.

You come from somewhere,
the omnipresent spirit... wrap that shawl around
my shoulders…
the warmth,
the comfort is immediate.

You are the spine of my existence,
the nerves in the fabric of my world,
the fragrance behind every bloom,

the roots that make me tall, anchor my being.

You are the healer of my scars and deep
wounds...
the simple balm for all sorrows…
You are the diamond of many facets
reflecting light on all my fragments… the
inspiration,
the muse of all my unwritten verses…

Behind the joy of my existence,
there is you the sustainer and
the anchor of all that is crumpled and wounded.
You hold me,
ready and steady me again and again...
to race with the wind.

(c)ketaki mazumdar

# My Winter Years

The ancient temples are full.
Sometimes worshippers wait outside
for Gods to finish their meals.
The flower vendors make fresh garlands and
prepare baskets of coconuts and garlands as
offerings.
In neighbouring churches, Christmas carols and
hymns are readied.
Candles and rosaries create their own
comforting aura.

I have often felt blessed in this coexistence.
My prayers bear fruit amidst sparkling festive
lights...
strung across borders.
My heart constructs peace,
packs them in gifts of tissues… delicate but real.
I release tension,

stay wrapped in inner peace... watch from
unknown doorways,
unknown people
murmur their prayers.
I watch a melting rainbow in the setting sun…
feel the golden threads descend to the beach, in a
stillness of perfection...
A year slowly winds down…
prepares for a metamorphosis...
and I withdraw like nature into a crucible of
waiting...
carry with awe the wonder of winter years…
and a rosary of tolerance amidst temple bells.

(c)ketaki mazumdar

# A Rain-Soaked Sky

I wait
For the sparks to catch life
on the dying embers...
I believed
in the fire of creation,
in the hidden colours of red and orange,
of glowing yellow,
of searing white...
streaks of an alchemy pouring out of
never-before-seen emerging hidden colours of
the mind.

The heat builds up, relentlessly stoking
the reality of a bubbling cauldron...
elevating, creating needs...
in a heady mix...
rainbows rising out of glowing amber clouds of
steam...
in a release...
I trail their curls into a lush space...

Why is life so mysteriously beautiful...
moulding bits of heady mixtures...
into a flowing stream…
releasing the aromas of Earth's internal creations
into my heart...
into a rain-soaked sky...?

(c)ketaki mazumdar

# Tomorrow

What I can give you will decide my journey…
How you love,
will decide yours...
for I will give you respect and care...
in promises
around the fire,
in seven steps of a sacred dare…
In my acts of love...
I wrote my rules with trust and care...
with phosphoric ink...
to glow forever as I lit the wick,
rang the bells and fragranced the air with the
purity of sandalwood.

In the debris of your looks,
in the sneer...
you flung the respect,

you flung away caring that was pure and
unselfish.
I was never the priority.

I swirled in a grey fog, unappreciated…
Like chess pieces tumbling, breaking bit by bit,
wounded.

You broke me... it was my past.
mistrust was my name...
in tinges of now, I rose...
it is my now, my future.

Hidden somewhere behind fireflies...
I was the light
for someone else.
Hurt and happiness
were bound together...
walked forward,
hand in hand.

(c)ketaki mazumdar

# God Paints

Sometimes in the fault lines of my heart
wildflowers bloom
through cracks and crevices,
from darkness
they struggle to rise
towards the gold light above
and the blue sky that spreads her silky tapestry.

The mindful wind caresses…
as God paints…
and love is an easy brushstroke...
the butterflies are unashamed. Embraces with
vibrant tenderness... longing
the tiny raindrops to descend on velvet petals.
Love embraces this longing randomness,
this unstoppable insanity of attracting
naturalness...
in a universal communication of completeness...
like a river that flows and embraces every bend,

like the bird, excited about her flight, loving her
freedom...
like the earth and sun's slow dance of passionate
attraction...
like the playful raindrop and light-loving,
uniting into a rainbow.
Wildflowers forget their struggles…
strain to catch the love tunes of this unknown,
in a mix of marigold dust and scarlet sunsets.

(c)ketaki mazumdar

# I Gave Away All

the light is dim
you cannot see me
for I am hidden
in the deep recesses of your heart
in the fold of your arms, in the hidden well of
your reflective eyes...
just a tiny pebble plummeting...
a sound echo…
in your quietly beating waves of breathing...

each perfume I wear
intoxicates your senses
am woven there...
in your pulse
your very life...
…am there…
different shades,
textures, aromas

am inseparable…
merged in the corner lines of your smiles…
at dawn and dusk, in the very flight of your
thoughts...
am hidden…
in a transparent casket of love...
in the very essences of thoughts, body and soul...
deeply etched in meanings…
in the pulse and notes of life rhythms...
am part of your strength and vulnerability...
a part of trust...
a magical alchemist,
a mystic empath...
who gave away all...
to be woven into you.

(c)ketaki mazumdar

# Summer Wine

The hues of summer drape the days.
My headscarf is dyed with such glorious
colours.
Ecstatic eyes are open wide… devouring flowers
and fruits.
The profusion of buds reminds me of life and
youth... and summer wine.

Kaleidoscopic fields of golden lyrics spread joy
and music.
I recall again and again all that is bursting with
energy and beauty.
The earth has bloomed again.
I drink summer wine and celebrate...
the tenderness of cool dewdrops and resplendent
dawns.
The early morning breeze carries secrets from
other lands, whispers to me.

The noon cauldron burns.

Crimson Palash flowers blaze, unfazed by the
heat.
Patches of shades are the saturation of gentle
leaves, where I wait for you.
Where we drink, on a carpet of flowers,
our sweet Summer wine.

The koels sing their secrets, echoing ours.
We watch the golden laburnum hang
resplendent…
passionate and feverish.
Unimaginable love spreads her mulmul cool
cape
hiding the smiles we shared between us.
Our eyes shone and said yes to the glory of
summer and her vibrancy.

We chose happiness and brilliant colours and
nature's textures and sweetness.
We were satiated by the languidness of jewelled,
maroon, summer wine.

The stars were brilliant in the night sky.
We drifted in the swirls of Van Gogh stars...
dreamt with our heartbeats, discovered feelings
and endless possibilities.
We lived in poetry... and words of love.
Summer gold and night velveteen blues,

in roseate dreams that were fragranced sweetly
with ecstasy.

(c)ketaki mazumdar

# Tender Words

breathless beauty
poised, awed
I wait
crystal dewdrops
to form
magical words...

pen poised,
shivering blue petals mesmerised
tasting
gentle, quivering love...
one dawn at a time…

awed stillness, nerves, shocked, moments of
pleasure,
poised promises,
a drop splatters…
dissolves

a burst of tender words...

(c)ketaki mazumdar

# Live Now

I pack my dreams into the deep pockets of my
jeans...
for today, the birds keep chirping and calling…
It's Spring!
I sing with joy...
my head is light and happy.

The wind whispers in my ear...
stop dreaming,
come dance with me.
Splash and swim in the stream,
pick pretty pebbles and smooth stones...
touch, hold and feel.

I take off my shoes,
put aside my cup of tea and walk on soft grass,
wriggling my toes delightedly.
I pick wildflowers for you and me.
I walk on the soft, squishy mud by the stream,
which will one day be a river.

On soft, crunchy leaves tiptoe...
watch the sun glimmering sparks like
candlelight... flickering,
making shadows of light and dark...
I dance into the stream,
splashing delightedly, watching the droplets of
water, like diamond jewellery, glittering.
The dragonfly wings… stretched, gleaming,
iridescent as the sun's light filters through them
joyfully… fascinates me.
Nature's jewellery beckons me... ruby red and
gold, silver dew drops, green, emerald leaves,
entices me into reality.

(c)ketaki mazumdar

# Little Joys of Life

Butterflies come to mind...
immediate joy spreads.
My soul is happy...
like a sunflower, generating energy.
Ordinary, everyday little commonplace joys…
transforms me...
and every time my love is different,
my joys tinged in new colours...
of happiness... uncomplicated and simple.

I float... feel unstressed,
on a calm world… draped in foggy rain clouds
that gather.
I hear the first growl, and I feel the first
raindrops...
the first jasmine's bloom and I embrace the
fragrance,
like a long-lost friend returning.

I sail my first paper boat filled with flowers,
let it sail with the message of love and hope and
peace.

Summer, with its first lick of golden mangoes...
the first sweet cry of a koel...
the Flame of the Forest... bloom.
Little joys that are free and bring the deepest of
intense happiness.

The skin of a night sky studded with stars…
my own special dome of wonder... as I lay in the
verandah...
and raise my eyes to the magnificence spread
above...
little joys...
when thoughts of love float in and out,
I know my life is turning inside out and upside
down...
I am loved...
that itself is a little bit of secret joy...
nurtured lovingly.

(c)ketaki mazumdar

# When Least Expected

My world is often mixed up.
Sometimes, out of the blue,
when least expected,
love drops in, unannounced,
in uncanny, unconditional weaves,
meant just for me.

There, when needed the most,
are the hands that reach out
in a warm embrace of comfort,
who understand the hidden needs often unsaid...
Suddenly, a smile appears,
chases away the greys and blues.

My world is so often just mixed up!
You walked in when the rest of the world walked
out.
All things broken are mended suddenly and
strong bonds are formed,
out of the blue,

thanks to the unexpected 'you'!
Storms subside, there is a calm and I'm
comforted, content,
like a Christmas gift in the monsoon!
You bring out the magic in me.
Just out of the blue...
when least expected... am born again!


(c)ketaki mazumdar

# I Am Content

Today I catch the pattern of your silence...
It's tone,
It's poignancy,
It's intensity... It enters my body, my soul, my
consciousness…
I sit still…
Like a pigeon, cosy in the first-morning sun...
sunbathing,
eyes gently shut.
In stillness.
Content in the space.
Just being.

You and I together, just being...
We embrace the silence.
Look deep and listen to our inner
conversations...
Hug deep the thoughts of compatibility...

while the grass grows,
hearts beat,
flowers grow,
butterfly wings flutter silently with an inner joy,
clouds float…
the soft winter sun glows.

We share our silence.
The story unfolds inside.
I know and believe too that blessings dwell like
dew drops, in silence...
and in the overflowing fragrances around,
in the rising swirl of sandalwood smoke,
in the last of the Autumn leaves, twirling down
in silence...
scenting their own secrets of waiting.
I am content.

(c)ketaki mazumdar

# In My Eyes

I hold you in my eyes.
You are the meaning of my life and every
moment seems new,
as you play your flute.

Sweet love of longing,
I feel the yearning,
to be with you always.
This beautiful full moon night as we swing
entwined,
with flowers, the stars, the peacocks,
the night and dawn breeze caresses,
fragrances the air,
as we exchange our garlands…

The music of endearing sweetness touches me,
teases me,
lets me know you are always there,
that the music you play is only for me.

You travel my curves with your music.
My long hair is decorated with mogra and
jasmine for you.
Your celestial music touches my shoulders, my
lips, my waist,
with the attar of madness.
I share my secrets with you.
The anklets jingle their dance...
I am in a trance,
while I hold you in my eyes.


(c)ketaki mazumdar

# Timeless

Sometimes his needs were like a dark, intense
sky.
While hers was the splashed freshness of lime
and eau-de-cologne...
Between them was desire.
The North Wind and the North Star were part of
their midnight tryst...
Reflected, shone, caressed, played on shoulders,
neck, lips and limbs.

The blazing, shooting star of romance,
rekindled,
like ember sparks on a trail of stardust.
Their sighs synchronised with the hum of a
nocturne moonlit world...
Their nights of pleasure were timeless.

(c)ketaki mazumdar

# The Nameless

Often, in a corner of my world,
I hear the gentle lap of the ocean in my soul.
Feel the sudden ray,
the sudden splash of spray,
her blessing...
know somehow that, as a woman,
I was made a mystery,
like the ocean near me,
always internally churning,
feeling deeply,
loving fiercely and balancing on moonbeams...
always being searched and searching.

Today I bow down in my journey.
In my search, I found the spirits,
the unsung,
the unknown...
the strong,
the foundational beams never revealed,
whose tears flowed internally, while they smiled.
I bow to their steely courage,

soft yet powerful.

It's not the ones with flowers and chocolates and
accolades of beauty.
I bow to the ones with grit... and no hope.
There are many.
They push the cogs of their own life,
fingers blistered and bleeding,
push bit by bit,
pain by pain,
wrinkles growing,
untimely thinning grey hair and stained,
shadowed skin...
and deep, cave-like eyes.

In their static world of sameness… unfree...
with unseen strength that does not allow them to
break free.
Strength and compassion, soft and powerful,
they hold up the tilting wall,
plug the vessels,
strive on without rest.
I bow to those hidden streams flowing with
debris, rocks, shards of painful glass, painful
pebbles.
Their amazing strength, unseen below,
unsung, unknown.

(c)ketaki mazumdar

# Always A Woman

she feels like a woman…
broad hipped.
encased in a lilac whisper of gentleness.
shoulders spread to carry the weight of the
world...

her eyes penetrate to mystical depths…
to far away vastness…
her heart now is filled with erratic beats...
lacerated with love and loss...
she is often in purgatory...
but rises, each time with phoenix wings…
purified by fire.
undefeated

she is a beautiful woman with clairvoyance,
entangled in stars,

moved by their vibrations, tunes and
criss-crossing journeys…
amaranthine glistens...
she feels like a woman.
always enthralling, still, calm and mysterious.
she is a part of celestial wonder...
her lips glisten, as do her eyes,
kohl lined around her wrinkles…
she is a woman...
draped now in the serenity…
of age and a never-dying womanhood.

(c)ketaki mazumdar

# The Jamun Tree

The Jamun Tree in the garden carries its own
ancient history,
its own summery energy and the story of its
glory.
Fertile, unbound, invigorating, bountiful,
the birds and the frisky squirrels dance around
joyfully,
happily drunk on its purple bounty,
soaking in the sonorous sounds of exuberance,
while the bees busily gather sweet honey from
the merry flowers.

People walking below her change,
become a part of her history...
but twilight, dusky pockets of love, gentle dawn
and the cleansing rain,
remain constant...
as does the music of the wind...
whispering stories.

My eyes create new images, new poetry,
as I sit in her folds...
dimensions of thoughts flow,
I feel the tanginess of savoured lips,
stained by squashed purple fruits.
I feel the tingling indelible,
the imperceptible, subtle nature's soul in my
heartbeats.
I feel the Jamun tree's seasonal change,
sometimes dead twigs and branches fall,
overgrown fruits drop to leave their mark on the
path below.

When I snuggle into her caring, loving lap,
I think and we feel alike...
we pause, breathe and sigh and spread love and
comfort.
We let flowers bloom,
fruits mature by the hot fingers of the sun...
listen to the songs of the birds and bees and the
squirrels' excited energy...
we converse…
the Tree and I and the rustling leaves of this
feeling,
alive, abundant, ancient Jamun Tree.
The season of summer love,
stains on lips,
on the ground below,

soaked with the fragrance and exuberance of
nature's truths...
deeply emotional custodian of my love.

(c)ketaki mazumdar

# A Front-Line Hush

Sometimes I dream of abandoned houses,
Blown up into bits and pieces,
windows wide open, with broken panes,
like painful eyes without lashes.
Once a familiar home...
my feet patter softly there, hesitantly,
on broken tiles and mud and mortar and grey
ash,
outstretched fingers separate the light veil of
cobwebs.
I try not to breathe.
Traces of the familiar remain in a corner of my
heart,
with the stench of the dead.

I walk into the torn tatters of longing,
sprinkled with heavy dust,
hanging there like misty shrouds.

Eyes burning,
they settle on discarded, misshapen pans and
kettles with holes.
Blue porcelain nights of pain and more.
I stitch myself, but the fractured, overturned
chairs…
their insides dismembered… cry.
Bits of shattered bottles and torn clothes,
broken toys and books and unmatched shoes
sigh.

The texture of memory is
pockmarked on broken walls.
They gather under the shadow of a pale moon…
with no stars.
Inside me are those who lived here once…
they have moved on and not left their pin
codes…
not even in secret pockets of overturned, cracked
flowerpots,
where once keys were hidden and accessed in
hearts…
Now congealed silence stains and
bittersweet pain remains…
breathless… with the unsaid.

(c)ketaki mazumdar

# In the Silence of Stars...

You look at me.
You are the twilight ether,
that I breathe.
You are the fragrance I wear on the pulse points
of my skin, and I feel.

You are the diaphanous cosmos... that I drape
around me.
We were born of stardust... shiny, gossamer,
precious...
that elusive magic of every twilight hour.

Your love is purity and the freshness of dawn...
I drink from that cup of dew and
the story of love embraces me.

Your love is the wonder,
the fragrance of night jasmine,
the garland of fresh, wet buds you placed,
around my flowing hair and my slender wrist.
In the essence of your love,

I drown.

I found you in the secret depths of the wild
Mahua flowers...
in the heat of summer,
drank of the nectar,
till I was drunk in the heady sweetness.
I could stay there with you forever.

You are every shade of colour in my life and
the translucent, windblown rain that makes an
ethereal melody...
Your love, I know, is deeper than the deepest
ocean,
Your waves... comforting
You are my beloved,
my handwritten poetry on fragranced paper,
that I treasure forever.
You are my meditation,
my supreme balance...
the whispered blessing.
You are the life,
my very soul,
my deep eternal theme,
my yearning.

(c)ketaki mazumdar

www.ingramcontent.com/pod-product-compliance
Lightning Source LLC
LaVergne TN
LVHW020334200726

843507LV00012B/2348